Minerals an

by Audrey N. Delmar

What are minerals?

Mineral Crystals

A **mineral** is a natural, nonliving solid crystal that makes up rocks. The salt you put on your food is a mineral. A metal fork is made of minerals.

Every mineral has crystals. Fluorite crystals are cube-shaped. Corundum crystals are six-sided. A mineral has the same shape crystals and the same chemicals in it no matter where it is found. A piece of quartz in Australia has the same chemical makeup as a piece of quartz in Arkansas.

Granite contains quartz, mica, and feldspar crystals.

Mica can form rocks that are brown or black.

Quartz is hard and glassy.

Feldspar is often white or pink.

Scientists have found more than 3,000 minerals. But only a small number of them make up most of the rocks in Earth's crust. These are "rock-forming" minerals. Most rocks are a combination of these minerals. Granite is made of quartz, mica, and feldspar crystals. White marble has only the mineral calcite.

Cinnabar

Orpiment

Pyrite

Mohs Scale for Hardness

 10 Diamond

 9 Corundum

 8 Topaz

 7 Quartz

 6 Feldspar

 5 Apatite

 4 Fluorite

 3 Calcite

 2 Gypsum

 1 Talc

How to Identify a Mineral

Scientists test different properties in order to identify minerals. Some properties they test are color, luster, hardness, streak, and cleavage.

A mineral's color is easy to see. Feldspar minerals are usually pink or white. But some minerals can be several different colors. Scientists must use other tests such as luster. The **luster** of a mineral is how its surface reflects light. Luster can be dull, metallic, pearly, glassy, greasy, or silky.

Hardness

The Mohs Scale for Hardness tells scientists how easily a mineral can be scratched. The scale is from 1 to 10. A mineral with a higher number can scratch minerals with lower numbers. Topaz is an 8. Quartz is a 7. Topaz is harder than quartz. It will scratch quartz.

Streak

Streak is measured using a special plate. A mineral is scratched on this plate. The color of the powder that it leaves is its streak. No matter what color a mineral is, its streak is always the same color. The mineral halite can be colorless to white, with pieces of yellow, red, or blue. Halite's streak is always white.

eral		Color	Luster	Streak	Mohs Scale
ite		Usually colorless or white	Glassy	White	2
blende		Dark green	Glassy	Pale gray	5–6
e		Gold	Metallic	Green-black	6–6.5
rtz		Milky	Glassy	White	7

5

How are sedimentary rocks formed?

Layers of Rock

Erosion is the movement of material such as rock, soil, shells, and dead plant and animal matter from one place to another. The material is moved by wind, ice, water, and gravity. It settles at the bottom of lakes, rivers, and oceans. It is called **sediment.**

Sediment is carried into bodies of water. Particles of sediment have different sizes and shapes. Some particles are smooth. Others are sharp. New layers build on old layers, pressing the older layers together. The weight of the layers bonds the particles together. They harden and form **sedimentary rock.**

Types of Sedimentary Rock

One kind of sedimentary rock comes from sediment of material that was once alive. Limestone is made of skeletons and shells of sea animals that lived long ago. Their remains formed layers. These layers are held together by dissolved minerals.

What kind of sediment do you think makes up a sedimentary rock named sandstone? Sandstone comes from pieces of quartz that are about the size of a grain of sand.

Mudstone is a third kind of sedimentary rock. It forms in lakes or oceans from tiny pieces of clay minerals. Mudstone is similar to a sedimentary rock named shale.

Conglomerate forms from round pieces of rock that are stuck together.

How Rocks Change into Soil

Water can drip into cracks in rock. The water freezes and thaws again and again. As the cracks get bigger, the rock gets weaker. Eventually the pieces of rock break. Plant roots can force themselves into a rock. This also can cause the rock to break into pieces. These natural processes are known as weathering. Weathering can wear away even the tallest mountain over millions of years.

Soil is made of tiny pieces of weathered rock. Soil also has dead and decaying plant and animal matter. Soil even has living things such as bacteria, fungi, worms, and insects. They break up the plant and animal material into nutrients for plants to use.

Weathering wears away these rock formations.

How Rocks Tell a Story

Sedimentary rocks can tell scientists about life on Earth millions of years ago. Scientists may find a 100-million-year-old dinosaur footprint. They may find a copy of a set of teeth from an animal that became extinct, or died out, 50 million years ago.

The footprints and teeth are fossils. Fossils give scientists clues about life on Earth long ago. Many fossils are found in sedimentary rocks.

Scientists get information from fossils. Fossils might tell how many legs a dinosaur walked on. They might tell what plants and animals looked like. They can even tell how Earth's features and environment have changed.

1.

The soft body parts of an animal decay after the animal dies.

2.

Sediment settles on top of the remains.

3.

Many layers form. Eventually the remains are replaced with minerals that harden into rock.

4.

The rock layers weather. The fossil appears at the surface.

How a Fossil Forms

Scientists can form ideas about Earth's history from fossils. They can tell when certain plants and animals lived. To do this, they figure out the age of the layer of rock in which the plant or animal was found. For example, ammonoids were sea creatures that looked like snails. Scientists think ammonoids lived from about 408 to 66 million years ago. An ammonoid fossil means that the layer of rock formed between 408 and 66 million years ago. Different layers of rock tell scientists how living things have changed.

Geologic Time Scale

Scientists have used their estimates of Earth's history to make a geologic time scale. The earliest period of time is at the bottom of the scale. The scale is in the same order as the layers of sedimentary rock. The layers with the oldest fossils are at the bottom. The newest layers are on top. The four major time periods are the Precambrian era, the Paleozoic era, the Mesozoic era, and the Cenozoic era.

Scientists use what they learn from fossils to make models of extinct animals.

Present

65 million years ago—Cenozoic era

248 million years ago—Mesozoic era

544 million years ago—Paleozoic era

over 544 million years ago—
Precambrian era

What are igneous and metamorphic rocks?

Igneous Rocks

Some rocks can melt. The layer of rock below Earth's crust is so hot that it is partly melted. This molten, or melted, rock is magma. **Igneous rock** is molten rock that has hardened.

Igneous rock forms above or below Earth's surface. Sometimes magma bursts out of a volcano in hot, gooey clumps. Magma is called lava when it reaches the surface. Lava may flow from a volcano as a hot river. Lava on Earth's surface cools quickly. It may harden into igneous rock in just a few days. Igneous rock that cools very quickly does not form many crystals.

Magma usually rises slowly to Earth's surface. It fills in cracks in the crust. As it slowly cools into rock, large crystals form. This slow cooling can take more than a million years!

Basalt is the most common quickly cooled igneous rock. Most of the ocean floor is basalt.

Gabbro cools slowly. The minerals in it may separate into layers.

The Giant's Causeway

A causeway is a road built above water. It is built on pillars. These basalt pillars are called the Giant's Causeway. The tops of these pillars are stepping stones that lead to the sea. There are about 40,000 of these columns. They are located in Northern Ireland. The pillars formed between 50 and 60 million years ago. Lava cooled quickly when it reached the sea. It squeezed together. Cracks from the top to the bottom of the rock formed these pillars. Many of the pillars have six sides.

Metamorphic Rocks

Rock is under pressure below the surface of Earth. It is squeezed by the weight of other rocks. This can cause rocks to change form. Rock that has changed as a result of heat and pressure is called **metamorphic rock.**

Metamorphic rock can form from sedimentary, igneous, or other metamorphic rock. Limestone is sedimentary rock. It can become the metamorphic rock marble. Rock can change form more than once.

Rock can change in many ways as it becomes metamorphic rock. Heat and pressure can cause the rock's mineral crystals to change. They may form again with new crystals of different sizes and shapes. The heat and pressure can also cause minerals to form parallel layers. This means some metamorphic rock may chip into flat sheets and slabs.

Phyllite forms from sedimentary rock. Its minerals are layered.

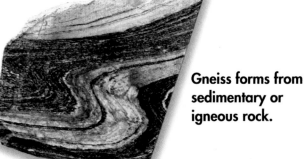

Gneiss forms from sedimentary or igneous rock.

The Rock Cycle

The rock cycle is the recycling of old rock into new. It is an ongoing process. The rock cycle needs forces such as heat, pressure, chemical reactions, weathering, and erosion. All three kinds of rock can change from one form to another. Not all rock completes the entire cycle. Rock deep in the crust may never reach the surface. It may never change. Sedimentary rock can melt and harden into igneous rock.

Slate is a metamorphic rock. It forms from shale, a sedimentary rock. Slate and shale can wear away to form new layers of sediment. These layers can harden into sedimentary rock. Rock under Earth's surface can melt and then form igneous rock. Over time the same materials can change into different types of rock.

The metamorphic rock slate forms from the sedimentary rock shale.

Glossary

igneous rock   rock that forms from cooled
                      molten rock

luster   a measure of the way the surface of a
                      mineral reflects light

metamorphic rock rock that has changed as a result of
                      heat and pressure

mineral   a natural, nonliving solid crystal that
                      makes up rocks

sediment   the eroded material that settles at the
                      bottom of lakes, rivers, and oceans

sedimentary rock rock that forms when layers of
                      sediment particles harden